CHANGING THE GUARD

CHANGING THE GUARD

PREPARING THE INTELLIGENCE AND NATIONAL SECURITY COMMUNITY FOR THE GENERATION Z OFFICER

JANNA SCOTT-TARMAN

Archway Publishing books may be ordered through booksellers or by contacting:

Archway Publishing
1663 Liberty Drive
Bloomington, IN 47403
www.archwaypublishing.com
844-669-3957

ISBN: 978-1-6657-3814-9 (sc)
ISBN: 978-1-6657-3816-3 (hc)
ISBN: 978-1-6657-3815-6 (e)

Library of Congress Control Number: 2023901843

Print information available on the last page.

Archway Publishing rev. date: 03/03/2023

This book is dedicated to the man who secured my heart and the Gen Z'er who inspired it.

- - - - - - - - - - - - - - - - - - - -

Editing support provided by
Alicia Hawley Rich and Stephani Johnson

Gen Z insight provided by
Tabatha Tarman and Evelyn Rich

Cover design by Caitlyn Zapata

CONTENTS

PROLOGUE

On September 11, 2001, colleagues became bodies. A year later I joined the intelligence and national security community, determined not to lose another.

— — —

This colleague-driven focus has sustained my twenty-year career within national security. In 2017, I was honored to receive the Intelligence and National Security Alliance Joan A. Dempsey Mentorship Award—an annual achievement award recognizing a member of the US national security community for their efforts to develop the future workforce. My acceptance speech follows.

> One ordinary morning in September of 2001, I was riding the Washington, DC, subway on my way to law school at George Washington University. I had just finished a summer internship inside the Pentagon with the Defense

Intelligence Agency and was only a year away from completing my final year of law school and realizing my dream of becoming an international law attorney.

I was stepping out of the subway car and onto the platform when over the intercom the station manager said something akin to, "The Pentagon station is closed due to an attack." It was September 11, 2001.

I froze. I had one foot in the subway car and the other on the platform, and I was locked in indecision. I could go left and have my planned day as a law school student, or I could go right and head to the George Washington University Hospital, because in addition to being a law student, I also had an emergency medical technician (EMT) certification.

I went right. I do not even remember making a conscious decision to do so. I just went right. When I got to the hospital, they were in crisis mode—throwing blankets on cafeteria tables to create makeshift beds and emptying supply drawers for easy access.

There was no time to change. I was wearing what I intended to wear to school that day.

One of the emergency room doctors hastened me to him, saying, "Janna come here." He took out a roll of masking tape and he put a strip of it across my chest. With a sharpie he wrote on me "EMT." He had me turn around, and he put two strips of tape in a cross pattern on my back and wrote "EMT" down both sides.

And that is it, that is my uniform. Seconds later I am in an ambulance off to have the worst day of my life.

It had been only days since I completed my internship at the Pentagon, and now I am returning as an EMT—as colleagues became bodies.

I knew then that I had to help and not just for one day.

Ironically, I was back working for the Defense Intelligence Agency in the Pentagon the day I received the email notifying me that I had passed the bar exam. That was supposed to be the defining moment of my life, and that achievement was supposed to be that which I valued most. But that day passed without notice because that achievement, and every award pinned to my chest since, has meant less to me than a strip of masking tape.

CHAPTER 1
EVOLVE—WE ARE THE DINOSAURS

The Generation Z population is roughly ten to twenty-five years old, born between 1997 and 2012. They will be the predominant new and entry-level hires to the intelligence and national security community, including our government, private, and academic organizations, for as many as the next fifteen years. They will also be the first new generation we hire en masse as we emerge from the global COVID-19 pandemic, which will drive their expectations of our community.

> Generation Z will be the first new generation we hire en masse as we emerge from the global COVID-19 pandemic.

United States military and intelligence elements draw their origins from the foundation of our country, and for just as long, the need for secrecy in our culture has kept our activities and communities behind locked doors with regimented practices and policies. Strict rules and restrictions on work locations, product storage, and communication practices dominate the work environment. This rigid cultural model has stood for decades. Generation Z may just be the generation to begin our evolution.

Generation Z is as diverse as any generation before them. They are not of one like mind, but they do share an incredible common history as children and young adults of the COVID-19 pandemic. While they will not all share the same ideas for how the intelligence and national security community should evolve, they will share the knowledge that it can.

Generation Z had a front-row seat to the upheaval caused by the COVID-19 pandemic. They used social media, online gaming, and global entertainment platforms to share and communicate world news. In the early days of the pandemic, just as the intelligence and national security community followed and attempted to assess the impact of the emerging virus, so too did Generation Z from behind their own screens and in their own peer communities.

My daughter was in the eighth grade in 2020. In late February of that year, she and her peers started to ask their teachers and administrators the same questions the rest of the world was asking. How can we protect ourselves? How long will it last? What happens if the school shuts down?

In those early days, based on the life history of all its administrators and advisers, the school reminded my daughter and her peers that a virus outbreak had never shut down the school for more than a week or two. Based on this comparative analysis, the students were told that this new coronavirus was unlikely to disrupt the school year in any significant way.

On Friday, March 13, 2020, my daughter's school began what was estimated to be a temporary, short-term closure. The students went home believing they would see each other again in one week, maybe two. My daughter, like so many of her Generation Z peers across the nation, would not see the inside of a school building again until August 2021, seventeen months later.

According to the U.S. Census Bureau, "Nearly 93% of households with school-age children report(ed) some form of distance learning during COVID-19."[1]

The vast majority of US Generation Z students began the 2019–2020 school year in packed classrooms in traditional school buildings. They were advised by their school administrators, parents, and community leaders that this was how school life has been for generations and how it would work for generations to come. A few months later, despite these assurances and decades-long historic precedence, with little warning and even less planning, Generation Z took part in what might be the greatest adolescent cultural and educational experiment of our time—mass virtual public schooling.

The implementation, successes, and failures of virtual schooling were as varied as our country, but one thing was universal. Generation Z discovered that wholesale and rapid change to American institutions and decades-long practices is possible.

> Through mass virtual public schooling, Generation Z discovered that wholesale and rapid change to American institutions and decades-long practices is possible.

Some Generation Z students still have not returned to a physical school building, some never will, and some never left, but every student was in some way affected by this pandemic. A generation whose entire educational career was turned upside down is unlikely to meekly accept arguments such as "This is how it has always been." Nor will they accept "That is just not something a large American institution or enterprise can flex to do."

While Generation Z endured upheaval in their education, they also continued their national and global communications and observations online, made even easier now with the hours spent on computers during virtual school. They had front-row seats for the unimaginable with lockdowns, closed businesses, and even medical and religious institutions limited in their ability to operate.

While much of the world shut down, Generation Z also observed how essential and necessary institutions adapted to continue the mission. In this, Generation Z observed their local and national governments operating at peak flexibility—an example of what is possible that they are unlikely to forget.

> In their most formative years, Generation Z observed local and national governments operating at peak flexibility.

Even within the intelligence and national security community, renowned for its rigid standards and security practices, Generation Z observed presumed impossible changes. Many elements went to mass and near total telework. Most of these employees were teleworking for the very first time.

As Generation Z enters our workforce, they will request flexibility in how they work, where they work, and on what platforms they work, because they know it is possible. Their expectations of agility will not just be reserved to their work environment. They will also expect agility in how we accomplish our mission to secure the nation.

Certainly, working in the intelligence and national security community is a privilege and an honor, and many will and should be thankful just to have a job in our field. I feel privileged to work here and am honored to serve alongside my colleagues, but there are many honorable ways to serve one's nation and family.

The most skilled members of Generation Z will have many career opportunities, including a wide array of professions that serve their country and community. They will have their choice of legal or medical careers, local law enforcement, charitable nonprofits, and teaching or lobbying, just to name a few. If we wish to recruit the best and the brightest of Generation Z into the intelligence and national security community, we cannot rest on the laurels that it is a privilege to be here.

> If we wish to recruit the best and the brightest of Generation Z into the intelligence and national security community, we cannot rest on the laurels that it is a privilege to be here.

We must resist the urge to call Generation Z's expectations disruptive or entitled—it is our time to evolve, not theirs. We are the dinosaurs.

We must see their expectations not as selfish demands but rather as adaptations and innovations—two traits that are renowned and sought after in the intelligence and national security community. Innovation is critical to mission success.

Adaptation in national security thinking and practices is necessary to find the next threat and thwart the next adversary. The intelligence and national security community will not evolve by expecting Generation Z to act and work like the last generation. We do not win the next war by planning for the last one.

> The intelligence and national security community will not evolve by expecting Generation Z to act and work like the last generation. Adaptation in thinking and practices is necessary to find the next threat and thwart the next adversary.

Tempering Generation Z's expectations of innovation would actually damage our national security mission. It would be the antithesis of progress.

Certainly, the intelligence and national security community should not discontinue practices that are truly necessary to secure our nation and its secrets. Being resistant to change, however, does not mean that resistance is necessary.

Not all calls for flexibility in our work models necessitate security considerations. Many will instead involve changes to leadership styles. For example, the greatest resistance to telework is often not for security reasons. Telework can be accomplished from alternative secure government locations.

Some elements of the wider intelligence and national security community have already reduced options for alternate worksites that were made available at the height of the pandemic. This loss of flexibility is not one Generation Z will accept lightly. They saw first hand through the COVID-19 pandemic how quickly our institutions innovated when forced.

We will demand that our new Generation Z officers innovate to protect our nation. If we demand innovation *of* them, we can innovate *for* them—in our leadership styles, our culture, and our antiquated practices.

> If we demand innovation *of* them, we can innovate *for* them—in our leadership styles, our culture, and our antiquated practices.

There are a limited number of assignments of such sensitivity or specialty that rigidity in work locations is necessary, but this is the exception, not the norm, especially for office positions.

Intelligence and national security community leaders must adapt. Our missions are varied and global, and the threat is ever evolving. If we want to attract the best and brightest of the next generation, we must be flexible not just in our mission, but in the way we lead.

We need this brilliant new generation in our ranks. As children and young adults, they saw their global and national leaders debating over COVID-19 restrictions and lockdowns, and eventually vaccines and the cost of closures. It motivated them to find creative and innovative ways to better their own lives and to take matters into their own hands. This unprecedented global event gave Generation Z an incredible aptitude for innovation.

Out of pandemic desperation, Generation Z achieved new and remarkable levels of communication and influence while still in their youth. They created online forums and organizations for pandemic-safe gatherings and took advantage of existing social media platforms to connect globally and in greater numbers. We will explore in later chapters how Generation Z has even supported the crowdsourcing of world-changing social movements.

Every generation begins with the benefit of the lessons learned and knowledge acquired by those before them. Generation Z has this benefit, but unlike multiple generations before them, they also have been driven by the pandemic to innovate in their social and educational lives, and they are emerging from the pandemic with a zest for life perhaps unobserved in such numbers since the days following World War II.

According to a Pearson Global Learner Survey, 72 percent of surveyed Generation Z students reported a "sense of urgency for completing their education" as they emerge from the pandemic, and Pearson's senior vice president for global corporate communications, Laura Howe, additionally noted that Generation Z shows "remarkable resilience in channeling their penchant for activism, creativity and motivation."[2]

In their most formative years, as the COVID-19 pandemic's global breadth came into view, Generation Z's world, their community, and their families were scared. Generation Z saw their futures to not only be uncertain, but unpromised. This has fueled their generation.

Generation Z's zest for life and ability to innovate, coupled with their knowledge that change is possible even in the most rigid institutions, fuels their possibilities. They will become our next greatest generation and one the intelligence and national security community desperately needs to meet our next national challenge.

CHAPTER 2

ELIMINATE ANTIQUATED PRACTICES

In the last chapter, we explored how Generation Z will be the first new generation that the intelligence and national security community will hire in large numbers as we emerge from the pandemic. They are also the first new generation to join our community on the heels of the global 2020 Black Lives Matter protests.

In addition, the population of Generation Z was roughly between three and eighteen years old when the United States Supreme Court declared that the Constitution grants same-sex couples the right to marry, and few members of Generation Z would have held any job predating the Me Too movement.

Many authors and articles credit Generation Z specifically for rallying people to action for the Black Lives Matter Movement in 2020. One such article by *Forbes* states, "Today's movement isn't only more palpable because of the widespread conversation happening on social media. It's the social media generation, Gen Z, that's using platforms like Instagram and Twitter as transfer points between thoughts and action, rallying people to the streets in the middle of a pandemic to push for policy change."[1]

These landmark social movements each had a unique and profound impact on the culture Generation Z inherited and grew up in. While the intelligence and national security community continues to address and evolve antiquated practices and norms developed long before these social movements, Generation Z will arrive at our industry knowing no other time.

While the intelligence and national security community continues to address and evolve antiquated practices and norms developed long before these social movements, Generation Z will arrive at our industry knowing no other time.

Like the rest of our country, Generation Z will not all be of like mind on these profound social issues and movements. They do, however, share a common history and life timeline in which these issues have always been at the forefront.

I suspect much of Generation Z will be surprised even by our recordkeeping. Many intelligence and national security community employment applications allow for only two binary gender options.

When our new officers are asked to further share their diversity data, they are often forced to choose from limited and narrow categories to define their own race.

> According to a 2021 study by the Trevor Project, as many as one in four LGBTQ youth identified as nonbinary.[2]

To safeguard and protect the nation's most sensitive secrets, the intelligence and national security community is careful to hire only those most capable of keeping those secrets. In doing so, the national security field has made honesty and integrity actual entry requirements, often with polygraph exams and extensive background checks.

If honesty about one's own self and history is to remain a required part of employment, then whenever allowed by law and policy, should we not ask our officers to tell us who they are in their own words, as opposed to asking them to select from government-defined options to describe themselves? Then, once our diverse recruits arrive, we must encourage and celebrate our officers for coming to work as their true selves and expressing themselves freely.

One of my most profound days in the intelligence and national security community started with a knock on my office door from a high-performing analyst. This analyst has won more national and agency awards than I will ever see and is an analyst that until that day I had only known as "he." This analyst came to my office to share that "she" was ready to come to work as her true self.

The inscription on the pedestal of the Statue of Liberty reads, "Give me your tired, your poor, your huddled masses yearning to breathe free." That is not just how we built this country; it is the only way we are going to defend it. If we are a country that is for "all," then we have to be an intelligence and national security community that is made up of "all" to defend it. This analyst brought us one step closer to realizing that vision.

> If we are a country that is for "all," then we have
> to have an intelligence and national security
> community that is made up of "all" to defend it.

In my twenty-year national security career, I have held many positions, including in counterintelligence, analysis, executive support, and compliance. I have served under many great leaders and had many role models, but of course, as in any industry, we do not always get it right.

Early in my career I observed a section leader inform his female officers that he would not select them for deployment to a war zone as long as he had male volunteers. Without shame, he said he would select "John" over "Jane" every time because he would not put a woman in harm's way.

His emotional need to protect "Jane" was more important than her dedication to the mission. If not for the intervention of other colleagues, that leader would have protected "Jane" out of her own goals.

Sometimes acts of bias are more subtle. I have observed young, brilliant female officers, the best and the brightest in their particular topic, prevented from presenting solo at high-profile events on Capitol Hill, at the Pentagon, or in the White House. In an act of perceived chivalry, leadership sent secondary and less informed officers to accompany "Jane" just so they were not sending her into a stressful environment alone. The result is that we protected "Jane" out of an opportunity to shine on her own.

In my home life, I find chivalry charming. Since the day I married my husband, I have not mowed a lawn, I have not carried a heavy piece of luggage, and I have not changed my own oil. I am sure this makes me two-faced as an advocate for women's rights. That said, I have no intention of disavowing my husband of the notion that I am too delicate for this kind of work.

Within the intelligence and national security community, however, we must take care that our notions of chivalry do not sabotage the career goals and aspirations of women in the workplace. In the workplace, chivalry must be about protecting a woman's goals and not her person, so that we never find ourselves protecting a woman, or any person, out of their own aspirations.

> In the workplace, chivalry must be about
> protecting a woman's goals and not her person.

Conscious and unconscious biases appear across the spectrum and against every sector of our diverse community. We cannot always predict when ignorance and bias will appear in the workplace, but we can be prepared to be strong when it does and to stand up for our colleagues of every generation. Most certainly for those of our youngest generation, Generation Z.

Generation Z will arrive at our industry with little to no work experience before global Black Lives Matters protests and Me Too. I fear they may already believe we are better than we are.

The intelligence and national security community certainly has come a long way. I can honestly and proudly recommend this field to all Generation Z aspirants, recognizing not only the exciting and worthy careers we can provide them, but also knowing how desperately we need their insight, innovation, and energy to discover and thwart the next threat. If we are going to recruit this next greatest generation, we must ensure we have an environment that is worthy of them.

For the intelligence and national security community, recruiting a diverse workforce and ensuring inclusion are not merely ethical and moral imperatives, they are absolutely mission essential. We cannot possibly prevent an attack from a threat vector we do not know, have never seen, and cannot understand. The best way to know it, see it, and understand it is to recruit and retain an officer who already does all three.

> We cannot possibly prevent an attack from a threat vector we do not know, have never seen, and cannot understand. The best way to know it, see it, and understand it is to recruit and retain an officer who already does all three.

To cover the spectrum of threats we face, the intelligence and national security community must recruit from within every sector of Generation Z. This includes seeking diversity in cognition and behavioral traits. A commitment to neurodiversity in our next-generation workforce could address critical gaps in both billets and talent. National security requires brilliant minds, and we have not done nearly enough to tap this reservoir of brilliance.

> A commitment to neurodiversity in our next-generation workforce could address critical gaps in both billets and talent.

The recruit we need, the one who has seen what we have not, is in Generation Z. We must find and recruit them first, and then maintain them by meeting their expectations of our work culture.

Generation Z will not be patient as we make improvements in culture and inclusion. They are the generation that saw, in their most formative years as witnesses to the COVID-19 pandemic and nationwide social movements, that wholesale and near-immediate changes to American institutions and decades-long practices are possible.

CHAPTER 3

PRIORITIZE MENTAL HEALTH

All generations have faced stressors and mental health challenges, but few so en masse or so recently before their onboarding into the intelligence and national security community as Generation Z. The global COVID-19 pandemic has been isolating, frightening, and long. The repercussions on this generation's mental health are only starting to be understood.

> In December 2021, the US Surgeon General provided this warning regarding the youth of the pandemic: "The COVID-19 pandemic further altered their experiences at home, school, and in the community, and the effect on their mental health has been devastating. The future wellbeing of our country depends on how we support and invest in the next generation."[1]

Mental health support is critical in the years following trauma. As we emerge from the pandemic, the intelligence and national security community must be prepared to offer mental health services not only for our current officers, but for our new Generation Z recruits. We must support one another in this community as we cope with the loss of human life as well as the loss of time and opportunities that resulted from COVID-19.

A year before the attack on September 11, 2001, I was in my second year of law school at George Washington University in Washington, DC. It was my dream to be an international human rights attorney, and I thought I might even get the chance to visit refugee camps around the world.

With this dream in mind and knowing refugees in times of crisis were likely to have more immediate medical needs than legal ones, I decided in tandem with my second year of law school to study for EMT certification through the medical school at George Washington University.

Just after that, during the summer between my second and third year of law school, I thought I could further prepare for a career in international law by working as an intern for the Defense Intelligence Agency inside the Pentagon. I knew, even then, that I could not understand or learn the nuances of intelligence law and international relations in regard to foreign intelligence without being inside the intelligence and national security community.

I truly enjoyed my experience as an intern. It is where I met two of my professional idols to this day, but at the end of the summer when they offered me a chance to stay full time in the agency, I turned them down. I had my whole life planned out. I was to be an international lawyer.

At the conclusion of my summer internship inside the Pentagon, I returned to George Washington University to complete my third and final year of law school.

Only a few weeks later, upon hearing of the attack on the Pentagon on September 11, 2001, I ran to the hospital and for the first time in my life skipped class. I thought perhaps I could help as an EMT.

I had meticulously planned out my entire life. What I failed to plan for was that as I entered the hospital that devastating day, I would be the only known medically trained person at George Washington Hospital to have ever been inside the Pentagon.

The weight of responsibility that knowledge and position put me in was not something I was prepared to cope with at such a young age, nor was the realization at the end of the day that I do not think I saved even one life.

I had my whole life planned out, but I am the 9/11 generation. Everything I planned to do with my life on September 10, 2001, seemed so much less urgent one day later.

It has been more than twenty years since that day, but in part because I did not get the mental health care I required in the months after, I still cannot get on an airplane, or in an elevator—because both feel like being trapped.

My husband works a late shift and when we were first married, he would come home every night and kiss me in my sleep. He had to stop, because to this day, if I am startled at night, I jump from the bed screaming. In one day, I lost a lifetime of goodnight kisses.

That is me after twenty years. So please imagine how bad my heart felt that first year after 9/11. I was an EMT who had just volunteered for the day. I was not associated with a regular firehouse or hospital unit. I did not have anyone to talk to on a regular basis who shared my experience. I was just a normal student, back in law school.

I had planned to do a great deal of public speaking as part of my legal career, in courtrooms and at international forums. In the days after 9/11 when I returned to complete my last year of law school, I additionally began to study in the evenings at the National Conservatory of Dramatic Arts, an accredited actor training program in Washington, DC. I had hoped the acting training would enhance my public speaking capabilities.

My principal acting teacher that year was a marvelous older woman. I can't recall her name, but her words may have saved my life. She said the "whole county is in mourning, and here inside the walls of the National Conservatory of Dramatic Arts, we are not going to suppress it." She said, "Feel it, express it, remember it deeply and authentically" so one day when you need it again on stage, you can access it. She gave purpose to pain.

For that crucial year my acting classmates and instructors became the group therapy I was not getting with other first responders. As we emerge from the pandemic, that crucial year is now.

The officers of the intelligence and national security community will need to become the impromptu "group therapy" for our teammates struggling to understand the pandemic. We will have to flex to support one another as we cope with the loss of human life, time, and opportunities we have all faced during this global tragedy.

> The officers of the intelligence and national security community will have to become the impromptu "group therapy" for our teammates coping with the loss of human life, time, and opportunities we have all faced during this global tragedy.

We will also need to encourage and provide professional mental health care when our informal efforts are not enough—and they will very often not be enough.

CHAPTER 4
FLEX TO THEIR LIVES

As shared in chapter 1, the most skilled members of Generation Z will have many options for employment, including many noble and honorable professions in service to their community. If we wish to recruit and retain the best and the brightest of Generation Z, we must be both a community honored for its service to our country and a desirable place to work.

> If we wish to recruit and retain the best and the brightest of Generation Z, we must be both a community honored for its service to our country and a desirable place to work.

At the height of the global COVID-19 pandemic, Generation Z observed their local and national governments function at peak flexibility. Even essential and necessary institutions adapted to continue their mission. Within the intelligence and national security community, many elements went to mass and near total telework status. As noted earlier, most of these employees were teleworking for the very first time.

> In March 2020, the US Office of Personnel Management, in anticipation of a potential federal office closure, called on all federal agencies to "immediately review their ... telework policies and ensure that written telework agreements (were) in place for as many employees as possible." They additionally called on federal agencies to "reassess their factors for determining telework eligibility to determine if additional categories of employees may be classified as telework eligible."[1]

Out of sheer necessity, the national security community developed remote teleworking processes and communication options in earnest. We uncovered novel and genius opportunities to continue the national security mission under unique and confusing circumstances. As we emerge from the pandemic, very little in the intelligence and national security community's practices and procedures appear impenetrable to change.

For those critical and specialized teams that could not telework, they practiced social distancing in ways never considered, with impromptu practices such as separate and distinct work shifts or makeshift construction of physical barriers to separate air between teammates.

As Generation Z enters our workforce they will expect flexibility. Many Generation Z officers will request telework accommodations to best serve their lives, knowing from the pandemic that it has been done. In the intelligence and national security community, at-home telework will not always be an option but telework can also be accomplished from alternative government locations as secure as one's home office.

Liberal use of alternative, secured telework locations can provide lifestyle, commuting, and family accommodations to our community's dedicated officers. This includes incoming Generation Z personnel who will have no experience in the intelligence and national security community predating the days of pandemic telework.

> Incoming Generation Z officers will have no experience in the intelligence and national security community predating the days of pandemic telework.

Planning as an intelligence and national security community rather than as individual elements could greatly multiple secured telework options. Multiple national security elements could build and share remote telework hubs in major cities across the country. These hubs could enable greater nationwide recruitment and the retention of both current and future officers whose life needs and desires take them outside our community's current work location options.

Many elements of the larger intelligence and national security community will or have pulled back from telework options that were made available at the height of the pandemic. This loss of flexibility is unlikely to endear Generation Z to our community. They saw the level of flexibility our community is capable of reaching.

If a fifth-grade public school teacher was expected to entertain, teach, and grade thirty students learning from their own homes during the pandemic, we can expect at least the same from an intelligence and national security community supervisor. Generation Z can and should expect a national security supervisor to be able to lead a team of dispersed adults.

Some specialized elements within the intelligence and national security community will not be able to take advantage of alternative secure work site options, but they are the exception. Resistance to flexibility must truly be for security and mission, not reluctance on the part of supervisors to lead personnel in multiple locations.

We cannot expect Generation Z to drop everything on our worst days unless we are willing to accommodate them on our best days.

As the intelligence and national security community brings in Generation Z officers in greater and greater numbers, we must be prepared to lead and motivate this new generation. This includes flexing to their unique personalities and needs. The level of talent, innovation, and enthusiasm for life this generation will bring to our community will be worth returning to the lessons learned in flexibility we uncovered during the worst days of the pandemic.

> The level of talent, innovation and enthusiasm for life Generation Z will bring to our community will be worth returning to the lessons learned in flexibility we uncovered during the worst days of the pandemic.

The need for adaptation will not only be in telework and work location options. The intelligence and national security community must also make allowance for "how" Generation Z approaches the mission work. The pandemic and lockdowns inspired a level of creativity and innovation in Generation Z our community has likely not seen before in large numbers among new officers.

> A 2020 Harris Poll found: "When asked about the activities, behaviors and conditions that help generations of people achieve peak creativity, this generation outmatched all others."[2]

A Generation Z officer does not need to approach a problem in the same way as earlier generations, nor do Generation Z officers need to communicate like us or work like us to be effective. Allowing these officers to work and communicate their way may prove more efficient.

Certainly, our Generation Z officers will need to follow the same laws and policies that govern the rest of us within the intelligence and national security community, but we can allow for flexibility in how they accomplish the mission within legal parameters. We must resist the urge to tell a

Generation Z officer "how" to accomplish a task. Instead, we should simply present to these new officers the task that needs to be accomplished and let them show us the way.

As global information systems have expanded, Generation Z has benefited with greater and faster access to worldwide information sources. Given the typical Generation Z officer's aptitude for publicly available data, telling a Generation Z employee how to find information may be counterproductive. Telling them simply what information is required makes a great deal more sense.

> Given the typical Generation Z officer's aptitude for publicly available data, telling a Generation Z employee how to find information may be counterproductive. Telling them simply what information is required makes a great deal more sense.

These changes may require adjustments to our traditional style of leadership, but they may be a far more effective and efficient way to manage the team that we now have in the game.

CHAPTER 5

PREPARE CREATIVE OUTLETS

The intelligence and national security community will seek to recruit the most innovative and creative minds of Generation Z. Only with officers creative enough to discover the unknown can we uncover and thwart the next surprise attack, threat, or disaster.

> Only with officers creative enough
> to discover the unknown can
> we uncover and thwart the next
> surprise attack, threat, or disaster.

If the intelligence and national security community treats our Generation Z new hires as we have the generation before them, then those we have recruited for office positions will be brought into mostly stale settings with either partial or full dividers separating individual workspaces in cubicle "farms."

National security threat discovery requires brilliant minds to think outside the box, and yet the first thing we will do to our new Generation Z office hires is place them in a literal box.

> National security threat discovery requires brilliant minds to think outside the box, and yet the first thing we will do to our new Generation Z office hires is place them in a literal box.

As the Generation Z recruit enters our secured facilities, we will additionally constrict their working environment with strict rules on communication practices and devices. Those restrictions will be followed by even more layers of security policies and practices.

Cube farms do not foster creativity but leaders can, and leaders in the intelligence and national security community must. It is a hallmark of leadership to be adaptable. If the mission requires creativity, then a leader of a cube-farmed team must provide creative outlets.

A few years back, I led a large team of defense analysts, all housed in a cube farm. Like most intelligence and national security community analytic elements, our work, while critical to securing the American people from outside threats, was heavily regimented by policy and procedure. As a result, the work environment felt stale.

We intentionally hired the most brilliant and creative minds to build this team of analysts. We needed them to make novel and unforeseen discoveries to secure against surprise attacks and threats to United States defense assets. Unfortunately, the cube office setting I had to house them in did nothing to foster the creativity our work required, and the strict but necessary rules on our analytic tools and processes further hampered creative problem solving.

I took the time to study the team and to consider what would motivate and energize them. One of the many things that I noticed was that every time I ventured into one of our conference rooms, I found small, often hidden doodles at the bottom edge of our white boards.

My colleagues, while sitting through staff meetings or training briefings, were drawing small creative images. They were quite amusing, as many of the doodles represented members of our analytic team depicted as stick figures on adventures in magical worlds, often represented as knights or superheroes.

Analysts stuck in an uninspiring building were doodling their daydreams of worlds and moments unencumbered by stale and secured facilities. These pictures appeared so often and so abundantly it was clear that art was an outlet for this analytic team. If used creatively, I hoped it could also be energizing.

On a day off I went to an art-and-crafts store and purchased more than a dozen white canvases, each about six feet wide. I brought them into the facility and hung them up on the walls around our office space. I also filled buckets with paints and markers and placed them in easy reach of the canvases.

I declared verbally first at a townhall and later in writing that the canvases were there as a creative outlet. I encouraged the analysts to take five minutes to doodle on the canvases to clear their minds, to break through analytic writer's block, or just to take a moment to think beyond our walls into the vast world we wished to protect. I further made clear my permission for the analysts to use these creative outlets by adding one of the first drawings myself—a peaceful mountain scene.

I took the small creative practice I had observed hidden in corners of our staff rooms and created an open and welcome addition to our work environment. This simple step added a few more smiles to our workforce and much more color to our walls. It signaled my encouragement that analysts in need of creativity in their mission products use art as a technique to refresh and clarify the mind.

The new art installations broke through writer and discovery blocks for many analysts. It was a successful tool to energize individuals, but I also needed to energize and motivate units of analysts to create energy that would motivate the entire floor.

Luckily for me, it was the last year of a major television series involving a fantasy world with warring clans, kingdoms, knights, and wolves, as well as the occasional dragon. It seemed every member of this large team was not only watching the show, but also breaking down each episode and predicting the next in ways only analysts can do.

The show had my whole floor buzzing, and much of the country as well. I can remember sitting in my office and overhearing analysts talking as they passed my door. Together they were recapping episodes and debating every detail of the complex plot. This conversation would be reimagined by dozens of different analysts over dozens of different days.

I sat down with a few of our most creative teammates on the floor. Together we invented a challenge based very loosely on the show. Our goal was to harness the energy and buzz surrounding the show and channel it into a motivation tool for our work products. We hoped to create a renewed fervor we could harness toward our national security mission.

We created a giant map of our own made-up world. We divided it into roughly a dozen kingdoms, matching the number of our analytic units. Each analytic unit was granted the right to name and rule a kingdom on our map.

We then created an elaborate set of rules and incentives for each analytic unit to build up arms and fortifications for their kingdom. At the end of the year the best armed and defended team would win the throne and the game.

Our incentives each matched our national security mission and work requirements. For example, a team that made an analytic threat discovery of such importance that it was read by the president of the United States would win a dragon sticker for their kingdom. A team that hired a new analyst who then passed their analytic certification exam would earn a knight sticker. We had a dozen or more similar incentives allowing our analytic teams to earn castles, catapults, and other elements required to defend their representative kingdoms.

All year our analytic units battled for rewards and fortifications for their kingdoms, each earned with analytic achievements and work products. The once stuffy environment was now alive with friendly competition.

There was never a lack of commitment on this team to protect our nation, but national security analysis requires creativity. The best work I have observed in this field has come from motivated and energized personnel. With this game, and the energy and creativity it brought to the environment, our team reached astounding levels of analytic achievement exceeding our own high expectations.

> National security analysis requires
> creativity, and the best work will come from
> motivated and energized personnel.

That year, we published more of the "top viewed" products in our agency than any other element. We impacted national security with new security initiatives, support to investigations, and in the fortification of defense assets, among other achievements.

Creative outlets worked to energize this intelligence and national security community analytic team. Creative outlets will be an even more necessary tool to energize our incoming Generation Z officers. A 2020 Harris Poll found that this generation might be the most creative yet.[1]

At home during the height of the pandemic, and even now as many return to school and the outside world, Generation Z has vast and real-time access to worldwide entertainment platforms. Entering intelligence and national security community cube farms, with their strict and regimented practices, will be an extreme adjustment for the Generation Z officer.

> Entering intelligence and national security community cube farms, with their strict and regimented practices, will be an extreme adjustment for the Generation Z officer.

For each Generation Z team and officer, the creative outlets that motivate them will be unique. The kingdom game my team played would not have worked for all officers and for all national security elements. Finding the right outlets will require adaptive and connected leadership.

Intelligence and national security community leaders must intentionally provide Generation Z officers with safe and secure creative outlets to keep their minds as agile and lively as we require them to be to secure a nation.

CHAPTER 6

WELCOME DIVERSE STYLES

The intelligence and national security community is composed of numerous government agencies and departments, in addition to private and academic partners, each with unique missions and tools. Each element has its own culture, and all officers have their own style.

> Each intelligence and national security
> community element has its own culture,
> and all officers have their own style.

The pandemic and lockdowns inspired creativity and innovation across the nation. Generation Z was no exception. Virtual schooling alone introduced much of Generation Z to new online platforms and opportunities for collaboration, which they used in inventive ways to continue to socialize with dispersed classmates. Welcoming these new officers will also mean welcoming their evolved and unique work and communication styles.

> Welcoming Generation Z officers will also mean welcoming their evolved and unique work and communication styles.

In chapter 5, I shared the creative outlets I provided to energize and motivate a large team of defense analysts. I hung canvases on our office walls to encourage doodling as a means of breaking analytic writer's block. I also led a year-long contest between our analytic elements based loosely on a popular television series with warring kingdoms.

With the contest, I hoped to harness the energy and buzz surrounding the show's final season and use it to create a renewed fervor that we could harness toward our national security mission. While effective for our team, trading analytic achievements for stickers depicting knights, fortresses, and dragons is certainly not what could be called a "traditional" leadership style in the intelligence and national security community.

In the middle of this year-long, epic analytic battle, a new executive officer was hired in the ranks above our team.

He requested a tour of our floor and to hear more about our mission.

I knew that when this new executive arrived, he would immediately notice our doodle-covered canvases and our giant kingdom map, as well as the stickers that were handed out daily for analytic successes. I hoped the executive would understand that analysis requires creativity; what may look like silly fun was actually a style of leadership.

While giving a tour to the executive, I shared our most recent analytic discoveries and the subsequent products we produced. Many had a direct and immediate impact on national security. As I spoke, however, I could not help but notice his eyes darting around, looking at the canvas graffiti on our walls and the stickers on our giant kingdom map.

I was nearing the end of my presentation and tour when two analysts walked around the corner and interrupted us. They did not know that I was escorting the new senior executive. One of the analysts blurted out loudly, "Janna, I think my kingdom should get a fortress sticker because we just briefed a national security director. Remember their kingdom [gesturing to the other analyst] got a fortress last week when they briefed an assistant secretary of defense?"

On display in front of this new executive were two adults passionately arguing over stickers for their fictional kingdom maps. My first thought was, "This is how I get fired." I must have been the least traditionally professional leader this executive had ever seen.

I am incredibly fortunate that he recognized that teams come in all forms, and what he saw on our floor was not wasteful nonsense but an energized and productive team, motivated by a leader with a unique style.

This supportive executive not only allowed our creative outlets to continue, but he claimed an island of his own on our kingdom map. Within weeks he was arguing for his own achievement stickers to fortify his island kingdom.

Intelligence and national security community leaders must intentionally adjust their styles to the officers they lead. The style that motivates and energizes one team will not be the same as the next.

It is not just variant leadership styles we must welcome and appreciate. With Generation Z we are likely to see wide variations in communication styles.

According to research by Roberta Katz, a senior research scholar at Stanford's Center for Advanced Study in the Behavioral Sciences, "Generation Z could learn about people and cultures around the globe from an early age, they developed a greater appreciation for diversity and the importance of finding their own unique identities."[1]

As discussed previously, our Generation Z officers will need to follow the same laws and policies that govern the rest of the intelligence and national security community, but we can appreciate and accommodate individual style in how they accomplish the mission within those legal parameters. We must also allow for and appreciate variant communication styles within our Generation Z population.

I returned to the Pentagon and the Defense Intelligence Agency a year after the 9/11 attacks after finishing my final year of law school. The first team I joined was charged with briefing the day's intelligence to a room full of military generals at four o'clock each morning.

For historic context, 2002 was an awful year to be in the business of telling anyone the day's news. The nation did not know where Bin Laden was or where the next attack might come from, and American and allied journalists were facing unthinkable atrocities abroad.

While most of the briefers remained stoic in the military style when delivering these briefings, I communicated authentically with emotions the way I learned while studying at the National Conservatory of Dramatic Arts. If the intelligence was devastating, I cried. If it was frustrating, I yelled. I can't tell you how many briefings I gave at four o'clock in the morning with a tearful lump in my throat.

As it turns out, one rises quickly in the business of intelligence by standing in front of a group of strangers, in this case military generals, and boldly and authentically telling the truth. Those generals remembered what I said because they felt what I said.

> One rises quickly in the business of intelligence by just standing in front of a group of strangers and boldly and authentically telling the truth.

My communication style was not the norm the day I entered the intelligence and national security community. Nor will the communication styles of many of our Generation Z officers be the norm. But authenticity will win the day.

To cover the spectrum of threats we face, the intelligence and national security community must recruit and retain a diverse and brilliant workforce. One style will not fit all, and one style will not secure all.

> One style will not fit all, and one
> style will not secure all.

We will recruit from the Generation Z population because we need their innovation, talent, and knowledge. Their diverse styles and way of thinking are exactly why we need them. We must not only tolerate how Generation Z uniquely approaches the mission but welcome it.

CHAPTER 7

RETHINK MENTORSHIP

The only good thing about a midlife pandemic is that you have a lot of free time to think about where you are, how you got here, and who to thank for it. I have more mentors and leaders to thank in the intelligence and national security community than I could even begin to remember.

I have been mesmerized my entire career by the strength and groundbreaking efforts of the national security officers senior to me. I have learned a great deal from the examples they set and from the stories they have shared from before my time. Their "war stories" demonstrated their expertise, and I believe the events in their stories made them leaders.

In much of the intelligence and national security community mentorship follows a common model. A member of a younger generation is paired with a member of an older generation. Together they sit down at a designated time and at a designated spot. The older generation "mentor" shares words of wisdom learned in past years in the national security field with the "mentee." The mentor additionally offers career advice based on the same past experiences.

Often these formalized mentor sessions dissolve into the mentor telling stories of life before the mentee's time in the community. These are war stories meant to impart wisdom. This mentorship model has and will work for many, but Generation Z's entrance into our community offers an opportunity for us to rethink the traditional model.

> Generation Z's entrance into our community offers an opportunity for us to rethink the traditional mentorship model.

Generation Z will enter the intelligence and national security community with a unique perspective and a common experience. They enter our community with their own painfully recent war stories as the youth of the global COVID-19 pandemic.

Much of Generation Z was in school when the world shut down. Many, like my daughter, spent seventeen months or more without seeing the inside of a school building. From behind their iPads and earbuds, Generation Z had a front-row seat to the pandemic's devastating reach.

Collectively, Generation Z lived through dramatic, uncertain, and world-changing times. The traditional method of mentoring new national security officers by sharing stories of past hardships may be less enlightening to a generation emerging so recently from a global economic, social, and humanitarian crisis.

> The traditional method of mentoring by sharing stories of past hardships may be less enlightening to a generation emerging so recently from a global economic, social, and humanitarian crisis.

All generations have faced their own tremendous challenges and hardship. But Generation Z did so universally, so recently before their arrival into the intelligence and national security community, that they are in a unique position as they enter our field.

In addition to the global pandemic, Generation Z has already participated in great numbers, and with elevated voices, in world-changing social movements.

According to an Edelman study, as many as 70 percent of Generation Z members are "involved in a social or political cause."[1]

In chapter 2, I noted Generation Z's role in rallying people to action during the global Black Lives Matter protests in 2020. Generation Z is additionally the backbone and impetus for the March for Our Lives movement to end gun violence in America. This movement began in 2018 with Generation Z largely crowdsourcing an entire social movement and rallying large portions of the nation.[2] Generation Z also has and will participate on both sides now that the Supreme Court has reversed *Roe v. Wade.*

The participation of so many Generation Z members in world-changing social movements also presents a unique twist on traditional mentorship. Generation Z has a real opportunity to mentor up to their more senior colleagues.

Many Generation Z officers will bring into our field experiences in community organizing and leadership, in virtual crowdsourcing, and with skills in numerous new and evolving communication platforms used during pandemic lockdowns.

Roberta Katz, a senior research scholar at Stanford's Center for Advanced Study in the Behavioral Sciences, shares that as children, Generation Z experienced "a world that operated at speed, scale and scope. They developed an early facility with powerful digital tools that allowed them to be self-reliant as well as collaborative."[3]

As both sides of the mentorship model have skills and war stories to share, we have an opportunity with the arrival of Generation Z to rethink mentorship. The future of mentorship may no longer be predominantly held in traditional and formal settings, where a more senior officer provides advice and guidance to a more junior officer.

The future of mentorship may be more organic, with less formality and with less of an assumption that the senior officer has the most wisdom to share. Leaders should seek to take advantage of teachable moments of authentic and unstaged connection when we can demonstrate leadership in action across generations and share lessons learned critical to the national security mission.

> The future of mentorship may be in taking advantage of teachable moments of authentic and unstaged connection when we can demonstrate leadership in action across generations and share lessons learned critical to the national security mission.

In life we often learn the most, and provide guidance the best, in unplanned, authentic moments. Everything I learned about patriotism I learned in one such moment.

As previously shared, when I arrived at the George Washington University Hospital in Washington, DC, on September 11, 2001, the facility was in crisis mode. The staff was throwing blankets on cafeteria tables to create makeshift beds and emptying supply drawers for easy access.

One of the first patients I aided following the attack was a young man who had been in a car accident. While not directly a victim of the attack, several accidents occurred near the Pentagon in the few minutes following the plane's impact, as drivers, in a rush to leave the area, were distracted by smoke and fire or the chaos in general.

This patient's injuries were significant. Most memorable for me was a bloody forehead and a severely broken leg. As I helped him into the emergency department, his eyes caught on the television images of the chaos that befell our country that day. It was perhaps his first glimpse at the chaotic scene as a whole, greater than his part in it. As I looked down to adjust the stretcher, the young man grabbed my arm.

He didn't know my name, nor did I know his. He didn't know I had skipped law school to volunteer, nor did I know why he was on the road that day. American to American, with his touch on my arm, everything else fell away as he said, "Please, don't worry about me, please, get to the people inside the Pentagon."

I have heard the term "patriotism" my entire life. I never truly internalized what it meant until that one unstaged, authentic moment—when a severely injured man asked the only person currently aiding him to leave and help his fellow citizens.

This moment transformed my national perspective. It also provided clarity on my new career path like no formal leadership or mentorship session ever could.

I have also had the opportunity to share unplanned and authentic learning moments within the intelligence and national security community. The first supervisory job I undertook was as the deputy chief to a couple hundred analysts. Being the deputy supervisor to so many was one giant leap into the world of supervision, but in this case the chief I worked for was fantastic. He was and is a great ally to professional women, and I knew I could learn a great deal from him as his deputy.

It turned out he had more faith in me than I had in myself. After only a short time together, he took advantage of a career-enhancing opportunity. He left on a year-long rotation out of the office, and I took over his position.

During the subsequent year, as I was still finding my way as a new supervisor in the intelligence and national security community, our team endured a heartbreaking loss. One of our combat veterans, like far too many combat veterans before and after him, lost his life to suicide.

> For information on veteran suicide rates, and to reach the Veterans Crisis Line, visit va.gov.[4]

I received the news in the evening and headed into the office in the middle of the night, unsure how to lead through loss. I had far too little supervisory experience on that day and for that moment.

In the middle of the night, and in an emergency, a formal sit-down session with a mentor to seek advice was not possible. I did not have a mentor available, but I did have a couple of hundred junior officers, all with much to teach and share with me.

One of the first things I learned early that morning was that the officer we lost had two best friends on the floor. They shared a meal together every day in our building. I feared they would discover their loss alone in the cafeteria.

I called them down to my office. We sat down together, and I told them that they had lost their friend. I can remember the shock and loss in their eyes to this day, and it broke my heart. They told me about their friend and shared stories of their time together. They cried, as did I.

I think it is particularly important when losing a friend to suicide to share and talk about your loss. The guilt and worry one can feel—wondering if there was a missed sign or opportunity to intervene—is painful and haunting.

I knew enough that day to know our team needed to talk to one another, but not necessarily how. So I asked the mentors I had available to me, the very officers I was supposed to lead. I asked for their suggestions on how best to inform the floor, how to present the news, and what additional resources we needed. We shared an authentic moment, mentoring and guiding one another.

Together we knew to ask our agency to provide medical professionals and counselors. The agency agreed without question and sent their best within only a few hours. We also decided that the full team should hear the news from me, but in small settings in which we could authentically share stories of our lost colleague and offer personal and genuine support to one another.

I next met with the officer's immediate teammates, including his supervisor. I shared the heartbreaking news that they had lost a colleague, and we cried together.

These scenes were repeated throughout that long day. This team needed to know, and then that team, until everyone on the floor had been informed by me, personally. I had now cried in front of a couple of hundred analysts.

This is not how I intended to lead that day, or ever, but it was genuine, and it was authentic. We mentored and supported across generations, and across teams, on how to both lead and follow that day.

The supervising office chief above me came down to check on our team. He sat in on several of the meetings I had with the analysts. He saw me tell them about our loss, and he saw me crying in front of hundreds of people.

At the time, I was the only woman who sat at his leadership table. I remember thinking when he swung by my office at the end of the day that he might pull me aside and say, "Janna, as a leader, and as a new supervisor, you need to be less emotional, especially during a crisis." Instead, he sat with me. We shared another authentic and unstaged moment, offering each other guidance on how to support the team in the coming days. We mentored each other.

A leader's principal and core job is to take care of their people. In the intelligence and national security community we must do so simultaneously while also protecting a nation. Sharing that essential mission with our new Generation Z officers will offer ample opportunities to take advantage of unstaged and authentic moments to demonstrate leadership in action, to mentor, and to learn from one another.

CHAPTER 8

ENABLE PERSONAL GOALS

As leaders in the intelligence and national security community, we often share with the next generation how we found success in our field. We tell them how we got to where we are and the hardships we faced along the way. It is a heartfelt practice, but if we are not careful we begin to assume that our career goals are theirs, and that success looks the same to them as it does to us.

Assuming we know and can intuit the career and personal goals of any member of a younger generation is folly. Assuming we understand Generation Z's goals could be harmful to incorporating them into our community.

Generation Z grew up in the pandemic, through improbable and unpredictable times. They saw entire industries, including our own, change their work models and practices near instantaneously. Their schools were equally impacted. What this generation knows and believes to be possible would have shattered our understanding only a few years prior.

> What this generation knows and believes
> to be possible would have shattered our
> understanding only a few years prior.

As we emerge from the pandemic, Generation Z's knowledge of what is achievable will drive their expectations not just of our community but of themselves. It will be up to Generation Z, as it was for the generations before them, to define their own "possible."

In the intelligence and national security community we have numerous career development programs of varying styles and success. Most are customized to their own agency or element.

The worst of these programs are built around the premise that we need to temper expectations and stringently reinforce traditional requirements to get from position A to position B.

If we built a career development program to prevent our newest officers from expecting too much too quickly, then it is not a "development" program after all. Life provides disappointments all on its own; we do not need to engineer a program to deliver the message.

> Life provides disappointments all on its own; we do not need to engineer a career development program to deliver the message.

The best career development programs in the intelligence and national security community begin with a conversation about the officer's personal goals, both near and long term. The best programs will not define what is achievable for the officer. Rather, they will lay out the available tools that the officer can select from—in training, experiences, and assignments, among others. Then the officer is empowered to merge the available tools with their own talents and innovations, to forge their own path.

I grew up in a rural town in Michigan with only one stoplight, and it was timed to turn off at night. Getting from there to here was not planned and was not controlled. No school counselor or career development officer gave me a map for this life, but they gave me tools, which, when combined with my own talents and life's twists and turns, brought me here and to my own personal goals.

If we listen closely to our officers, their goals are more specific and personal than just moving up the ranks. They will have personal career goals that include adventures, education, and skill development, each of which we might support.

> If we listen closely to our officers, their goals are more specific and personal than just moving up the ranks.

Early in my career I served as an intelligence liaison officer to Pentagon executives. One of the many tasks of an intelligence liaison officer is to arrive at the Pentagon at three o'clock in the morning to quickly absorb and synthesize the most relevant intelligence reporting and analysis from the previous twenty-four hours.

For my agency, this is a high-profile and career-developing assignment. I found myself in this position with little more than two years of experience. At first, I was sent there as an emergency short-term replacement for a colleague with a sick family member. A two-week assignment turned into a permanent position because I had an aptitude for the job.

I could read and absorb complex intelligence and analysis quickly. I could then present it succinctly and uniquely for each executive client, tailored to their information needs and schedule.

It was in my first year at this job that I became pregnant with my daughter. My timing was less than ideal. Morning sickness is bad enough. Morning sickness at three o'clock in the morning in the Pentagon is much, much worse.

The Pentagon is the world's largest low-rise office building.[1] I once heard the building contains more than 280 bathrooms. I am relatively certain that I threw up in every one of them—men's and women's. When you are that urgently sick, the little stick figures on the outside of the bathroom do little to deter your entrance.

I was so ill one morning that I even threw up in the middle of a sentence, in the middle of a briefing, to a deputy assistant secretary of defense (DASD), the equivalent of a two-star general. Fortunately for me, the DASD was kind and supportive and would have let me continue with the briefing if I had not been so mortified and insisted on leaving.

I still do a great deal of public speaking, and rarely get stage fright. When you have vomited in front of an executive, it is hard to do worse.

I was incredibly fortunate that year to have had great teammates in the intelligence liaison assignment who understood that each person's goals are personal and unique to them. They were supportive of mine.

If it had been up to a traditional career development officer, I never would have been in that position in the first place, and especially not after I became ill on the job. As I said, this was a high-profile position usually reserved for persons with far more experience than I had. My presence there as a new officer was not a traditional career path.

It was my personal career goal to forge on. I was good at it, and I was not going to be the weakest link on the team, even with morning sickness. I also think emotionally I needed to prove to myself that my becoming a mother would not alter my career trajectory.

My teammates that year are the reason I got through it. They understood that it was my personal goal to continue, even if it was not a requirement of my career nor a traditional career path. They never encouraged me to just go home or take another assignment. Instead, they gave me the tools that I needed (in one instance literally a vomit bucket), which I combined with my talents in order to survive the year and maintain my position.

Our incoming Generation Z officers will each come with their own personal goals and definitions of success. They know from the events of their formative years that even the unimaginable is possible.

It is not up to us as the leaders of the intelligence and national security community to define Generation Z's career path and options, nor to determine what success should mean to them. We are here to provide tools—education, assignments, and techniques. Generation Z will provide the talent and motivation to forge their own way.

CHAPTER 9

GENERATION Z TODAY

The oldest members of Generation Z are entering the intelligence and national security community, while their youngest counterparts are anticipating middle school. Many of our prospective Generation Z officers are purposefully and meticulously preparing for our community—with specialized academic programs, military officer training, or language immersion courses, among other and numerous options. Others, particularly on the younger side of this generation, are simply growing, learning, and experiencing the life lessons that may someday become critical to our mission.

Many of our future Generation Z officers cannot even imagine that they will find their way into the intelligence and national security community. I certainly would not have at their age. Still, their academic and life experiences today will someday soon bring new skills and awareness to our community.

> Generation Z's academic and life experiences today will someday soon bring new skills and awareness to our community.

Generation Z is currently learning communication techniques and programs, participating in global exchanges of information, and becoming expert users of technologies that were unknown only a few years ago. Many are also watching us. They are observing as national leaders share our successes and failures not only on the seven o'clock news, but twenty-four hours a day, seven days a week on screens that fit in the palm of their hands.

Our communities built brick-and-mortar schools to protect Generation Z from the elements. Their teachers and administrators established practices to protect them from intruders. The nation spent billions to protect their air, sea, and land. Their parents spent their entire lives protecting them from wall sockets, cars, wild animals, and fires.

All these protections meant very little when the threat came to their formative years in increments too small to see with the naked eye, and in the genus *Betacoronavirus*.

> The threat came to their formative years in increments too small to see and in the genus *Betacoronavirus*.

Generation Z had the choice to say that the young survive this virus so let the old fend for themselves. They had the choice to complain and sulk through broken school years. Many chose otherwise.

In 2021, I provided the commencement address for my old high school in a small town on the lower peninsula of Michigan. I met with a number of the students in advance, and I was in awe of how they did more than just endure and suffer through the pandemic. They stood up and showed up when much of their community could not.

In just one of many small community examples, in my hometown's class of 2021, the students shared with me that they earned enough from chocolate sales their senior year to donate nearly 700 holiday gifts to low-income families in their community. That is hundreds of kids who will forever remember 2020 as the Christmas with COVID-19 but were spared from remembering it as the year with no gift.

The class of 2021 also shared that they held food drives to stock the shelves of food banks facing record-breaking needs. They also passed out lunches to hungry kids with closed schools.

The local nursing home was devastated by the virus. These high school students recognized its walls to be filled not by nameless numbers, but by the very people who built, prepared, and sustained their hometown for their parents and now for them. Students flooded the nursing home with cards, notes, and good cheer long after its doors were closed for safety.

They used their technical skills to help their community by offering services to the blind through virtual apps. They assisted individuals without internet access by scheduling vaccine appointments. They monitored at-risk persons at vaccine clinics even before their age group was eligible to receive the vaccine themselves.

These stories illustrate the pandemic response of the Generation Z population of only one small town. We can multiply that across the country. As shared in earlier chapters, in addition to their pandemic efforts, Generation Z has additionally played significant roles in world-changing social movements.

Generation Z is coming quickly and as a group to the intelligence and national security community with a drive to make up for the experiences and years lost to the pandemic. Like every generation before them, Generation Z possesses an inevitable obligation to take their turn as our next global leaders. It is our obligation to prepare the way for them.

> Like every generation before them, Generation Z possesses an inevitable obligation to take their turn as our next global leaders. It is our obligation to prepare the way for them.

THE COLLEAGUES YOU KEEP

The purpose of this book is to prepare the intelligence and national security community for the Generational Z officer—our predominant entry-level new hires for as many as the next fifteen years. Preparing Generation Z for our field is a different story entirely, but as I have centered my career on supporting colleagues, I would be remiss not to provide a short note to our new Generation Z officers.

— — —

Generation Z, as you enter our field you will receive from your employer specific and advanced training on the skills, governing policies, and tools of your new position. This training will provide you the acumen you need to do your job, but it will be your colleagues who make your job a career. It will be the people with whom you serve who will inspire you, challenge you, and drive you to devote much of your life to our common cause.

I have found that my most valued colleagues fall within the following categories. No category is more important than another; all will inspire your growth and further your career within the intelligence and national security community. Seek out these colleagues as you join our field, care for them as they care for you, and protect our nation as you do.

YOUR OPPOSITE

Find the colleague who disagrees with you. No one will make you defend your findings more than your opposite. They will drive you to contemplate, rethink, and better sell your decisions and plans. Cherish their input. You and your actions will be better for keeping closest the colleague who disagrees with you the most.

Find the colleague whose leadership style, life experiences, and skills are the opposite of your own. There is no better addition to your team than the colleague who is the opposite of you.

Cherish the colleague who complements not your strengths but your weaknesses.

YOUR MORAL COMPASS

Find a colleague who will remind you why you joined the intelligence and national security community.

You are human. You will have dark days and dark times. You will have moments where it would be emotionally easier not to care, or when you are so buried in tasks and bureaucracy that you are annoyed by the very institutions and policies you chose to protect.

In these moments the colleague you need the most is the one who will remind you what it is all for—that we are here to protect the people and communities we love. This colleague is irreplaceable.

YOUR COMPETITOR

Find your peer competitor.

This is the colleague you will compete with for career assignments and opportunities, or perhaps they will be your counterpart in another agency or element that does things differently than you have.

Ideally, your competitor will be better than you in certain technical areas or will be someone setting and achieving loftier career goals than you have made for yourself. This competition will drive you. Your competitor's example may just be the inspiration you need to step outside your comfort zone and do more than you imagined possible.

YOUR MODEL

Find and observe your professional role models.

Find your leadership model, your technical acumen model, your emotional intelligence model, and all the other professional models significant to you.

Whom you choose and with what skill sets will depend on your career field and aspirations. When I first joined the intelligence and national security community, I was intimidated by the strict security and had anxiety about making a mistake. One of the first professionals I began to observe as a role model was an officer who demonstrated a firm grasp of the rules and whom I had heard providing notes on operational security in multiple team meetings.

I have collected many more role models with multiple professional skills and leadership traits in the twenty years since. Each person has enriched my career and my professional toolbox, many without even knowing I was watching.

YOUR NAVIGATOR

Your navigator will be both your cheerleader and your guide. This is the colleague who supports your professional transitions.

Find the colleague who will guide you in the big steps. For example, in your journey from officer to supervisor, your navigator will bolster your confidence and provide mentorship as you make your move.

Also, find the colleague who will guide your skill development. For example, find the person who will advocate for your voice and ideas to not only be heard in small staff meetings, but in front of hundreds and then thousands.

YOUR CHALLENGE

Welcome the colleague who will challenge you to do better and more, even when it is inconvenient.

Your challenge colleague is the officer who will walk into your office when you are already burdened with tasks and responsibilities and point out where you need process or tradecraft improvement. They will not be patient when change is necessary.

I find this colleague often in idealistic new employees. You will want to say, "Not now," or suggest they wait till they are in a higher position and can understand how much there is to manage. Resist the urge to put them off. This colleague is giving you an opportunity to outdo even your own expectations.

Your challenge colleague will come to you because they believe you can help. Prove them right.

YOUR DEFENDER

Your life and career will not be perfect. This is a challenging profession of high stakes and stress. You will not always be popular, and tough decisions will lead to tough moments.

The defender colleague knows your credentials and your history of dedication to the mission and the personnel that execute it. This colleague will speak up for you and voice an assumption of positive intent in your actions and decisions, even when your decisions are unpopular—even if you are not in the room.

This is not a "yes man" or a colleague who cosigns bad decisions. It is a person you can count on to assume the best of you when the job is the hardest.

MORE TO SHARE

I mentioned in chapter 3 that when I was in my early twenties and still in law school, I believed that I could not understand or learn the nuances of the practice of intelligence and the business of national security without being inside the intelligence and national security community. While that may remain true for the understanding of day-to-day activities and tasks, I now know there is much that can be learned of the larger picture of national security from openly available written and recorded resources.

I would encourage aspiring national security officers, and in particular the future Generation Z officers this book anticipates, to visit the public sites and networking pages of the intelligence and national security community. Our community includes a multitude of government agencies and departments, in addition to private and academic partners, each with unique missions, tools, and tasks. Each of their sites provide a plethora of educational resources, historical reference materials, and current hiring notices.

There are also alliances, advocacy groups, and private organizations that support the intelligence and national security community and its members. These groups provide learning resources and tools for current and aspiring employees, including education on the roles and missions of the community's elements.

Additionally, the list of recorded resources that provide information about the national security community grows weekly, particularly in the podcast arena. Both private and government institutions are telling the stories of our community through these digital series.

As for my individual efforts to encourage aspiring persons to join the national security field, several of my personal stories were previously shared for public release. A few examples are provided below.

I was featured in a *Federal Drive* segment on leading in the intelligence community. The interview was conducted by a reporter from Federal News Radio and includes an audio recording of the first time I told my 9/11 story in public.[1]

I provided remarks as the recipient of the 2017 Joan A. Dempsey Mentorship Award—an annual achievement award recognizing a member of the US National Security Community—from the Intelligence and National Security Alliance (INSA).

I was additionally honored to speak as a panelist at INSA's first "Empowering Women and Engaging Men" symposium.[2] This forum provided a public discussion on issues that women face within national security careers.

I spoke at events hosted by the group Amazing Women of the Intelligence Community (AWIC). AWIC is dedicated to the development of professional women serving the US national security mission.

I was a featured guest on the *Iron Butterfly* podcast.[3] *Iron Butterfly* is the first podcast by and for the women of the intelligence community. Each episode features an interview with an unsung heroine, presenting the stories and voices of women in the intelligence and national security community.

NOTES

Chapter 1

1 Kevin McElrath, "Nearly 93% of Households With School-Age Children Report Some Form of Distance Learning During COVID-19," United States Census Bureau, August 26, 2020, https://www.census.gov/library/stories/2020/08/schooling-during-the-covid-19-pandemic.html, accessed October 7, 2022.

2 Mark Perna, "How The Pandemic Is Inspiring Gen-Z To Rethink Their Education And Career," *Forbes*, July 27, 2021, https://www.forbes.com/sites/markcperna/2021/07/27/how-the-pandemic-is-inspiring-gen-z-to-rethink-their-education-and-career/, accessed October 7, 2022.

Chapter 2

1 Rebecca Bellan, "Gen Z Leads The Black Lives Matter Movement, On And Off Social Media," *Forbes*, June 12, 2020, https://www.forbes.com/sites/rebeccabellan/2020/06/12/gen-z-leads-the-black-lives-matter-movement-on-and-off-social-media/?sh=5646173719a8, accessed October 7, 2022.

2 "The Trevor Project Research Brief: Diversity of Nonbinary Youth," The Trevor Project, July 2021, https://www.thetrevorproject.org/wp-content/uploads/2021/07/Diversity-of-Nonbinary-Youth_-July-Research-Brief.pdf, accessed October 7, 2022.

Chapter 3

1   U.S. Department of Health and Human Services press release, "U.S. Surgeon General Issues Advisory on Youth Mental Health Crisis Further Exposed by COVID-19 Pandemic," HHS.gov, December 7, 2021, https://www.hhs.gov/about/news/2021/12/07/us-surgeon-general-issues-advisory-on-youth-mental-health-crisis-further-exposed-by-covid-19-pandemic.html, accessed October 7, 2022.

Chapter 4

1   Memorandum for Heads of Executive Departments and Agencies, "Coronavirus Disease 2019 (COVID-19): Additional Guidance," Office of Personnel Management, March 7, 2020, https://www.chcoc.gov/content/coronavirus-disease-2019-covid-19-additional-guidance, accessed October 7, 2022.

2   Khrysgiana Pineda, "Generation Create? Gen Z might be the most creative generation yet, poll says, *USA Today*, August 18, 2020, https://www.usatoday.com/story/news/nation/2020/08/18/generation-z-may-most-creative-yet-study-says/5589601002/, accessed October 7, 2022.

Chapter 5

1   Khrysgiana Pineda, "Generation Create? Gen Z might be the most creative generation yet, poll says, *USA Today*, August 18, 2020, https://www.usatoday.com/story/news/nation/2020/08/18/generation-z-may-most-creative-yet-study-says/5589601002/, accessed October 7, 2022.

Chapter 6

1   Melissa De Witte, "Gen Z are not 'coddled.' They are highly collaborative, self-reliant and pragmatic, according to new Stanford-affiliated research," *Stanford News*, January 3, 2022, https://news.stanford.edu/2022/01/03/know-gen-z/, accessed October 7, 2022.

Chapter 7

1 Corey Martin, "The Rise of Trusted Influence: 3 Key Gen Z Trends to Act On," Edelman, June 14, 2022, https://www.edelman.com/insights/rise-trusted-influence-3-key-gen-z-trends-act, accessed October 7, 2022.

2 For additional information on the March for Our Lives movement, visit marchforourlives.com

3 Melissa De Witte, "Gen Z are not 'coddled.' They are highly collaborative, self-reliant and pragmatic, according to new Stanford-affiliated research," *Stanford News*, January 3, 2022, https://news.stanford.edu/2022/01/03/know-gen-z/, accessed October 7, 2022.

4 For information on veteran suicide rates, and to reach the Veteran's Crisis Line, visit https://www.mentalhealth.va.gov/suicide_prevention/data.asp

Chapter 8

1 Claudette Roulo, "Ten Things You Probably Didn't Know about the Pentagon," DoD news, January 3, 2019, https://www.defense.gov/News/Feature-Stories/story/Article/1650913/10-things-you-probably-didnt-know-about-the-pentagon/, accessed October 7, 2022.

More to Share

1 To listen to this recording, visit https://federalnewsnetwork.com/tom-temin-federal-drive/2017/03/jana-scott-tarman-leading-in-the-intelligence-community, accessed October 7, 2022.

2 To watch this video, visit https://www.cybersecuritytv.net/Events/INSA_180501/VideoId/213/UseHtml5/True, accessed October 7, 2022.

3 To listen to this podcast, visit https://shows.acast.com/the-iron-butterfly/episodes/janna-scott-tarman-the-trampoline, accessed October 7, 2022.

ABOUT THE AUTHOR

Janna Scott-Tarman has a Juris Doctorate from the George Washington University Law School and a bachelor's degree from the University of Michigan. She additionally studied international law through an exchange program at Oxford University in England. She has served twenty years at the Defense Intelligence Agency. Janna has received multiple national and agency-level team awards for the protection of US critical infrastructure and the national defense supply chain, and she was the 2017 recipient of the Intelligence and National Security Alliance Intelligence Community Joan A. Dempsey Mentorship Award. Janna is married to Carl, a DC metro mechanic, and together they have a 16-year-old daughter.

author.changing.the.guard@gmail.com